Things I Should Have Said

Amjad K. Hajyassin

To Mama.

Mama's English

Her English came out
Of her mouth like
She was spitting
out shards of glass.

She spoke English
Like she had razor blades
Stuck between her cheeks.
Cutting the insides of her
Mouth, each word
Covered in blood.

Whenever she spoke
too quickly, the English
Came out like marbles
Falling to the floor
and she picked them
up along with her pride.

She spoke English
Because Americans
Spoke to her too
slowly.

She wanted them to
eat the words that came
Out of her mouth.

"Fuck you,"
Was her favorite
English phrase.
It came out like poetry.
It danced on her lips,
while her eyes smiled.

She spoke English.
But her Arabic was
my favorite song.

Five Stages of Grief

I. Denial.

I know when I get up
She's going to be
fine. She'll be
in the living room
watching old
Arabic sitcoms
and telling me to
get her the remote.
She's going to be okay.
She'll be here in the
Morning.

II. Anger.

Why her?
She didn't hurt anyone.
What did she do to

wrong you, God?
All the shit going on
in the world and you
had to take the one
Good thing?
Fuck you.

III. Bargaining.

I'm sorry. That was wrong.
I didn't mean it.
I'll do whatever you ask.
I'll pray 5 times.
I'll fast.
I'll be a good person.
Fuck it. Take my life
Instead. She's worth more
than I am.
Please.

IV. Depression.

It hurts so much without her.
I can't breathe.
I can't sleep.
The pain doesn't go away.
I don't want to be
on this earth
if she's not on it.

V. Acceptance.

You're okay, mama.
You're in a better place.
It's selfish of me to
want you here
while you're in pain.
I'll be okay.
I promise.

I'll be okay.

Tight-lipped

Alhamdiallah passed
between her teeth
like flash floods breaking
down dams and levees.

Insha'Allah spilled
from her lips like the
feeling one has while
waiting for spring and
the blossoming of flowers.

Ya Allah confidently
flowed from her mouth
like when the sun crashes
down against clouds.

Yet, these words stumbled
out of my mouth like
glass falling to the floor

shattering against stone.

Shattering against
"Alhamdiallahs" and
"Insha'Allahs."

Waves

I had a dream once,
where my mother was at
the beach, sitting on the
cold sand.

It was just after sunset,
when the sun shoots out
its last rays of light and turns
everything purple.

The waves kissed the shore
and ran away back into
the ocean. My mother was
staring out into the distance.

Habibi, she said.
I'm like the waves.
No matter how many times
I leave you.

I'll always come back.
You're my shore, habibi.

And she was always
my wave.

Earthquake

In 1994, the Northridge
earthquake shook
so hard, my mother's
China set crashed to the floor.

My mother grabbed
my brothers and I.
We hid underneath tables
in our small house
in the Inland Empire.

As the house shook
around us,
Her body was a
rock.

Sixteen years later,
my mother's death shook me so
hard
my knees buckled from
underneath me.

It shook me
harder than tectonic
plates shifting violently
under my feet

I still feel the aftershocks.

Footsteps

I want to follow
in the
footsteps of
my mother who
broke her back
Praying to God.
Chapped lips
Whispering
Prayers from
A Holy Book
that she took
as the
Truth.

I want to follow
in those
Footsteps.

But she was a
better
person
than I am.

Who is Worthy?

A man asked the Prophet,
Who is worthy of good
companionship?
The Prophet said,
Your mother.

She held me
close to her
longer than nine–
months. Her hands
were my Home.

The man asked, then who?
The Prophet said,
Your mother.

She wiped tears
from swollen eyes.
Prayed for me

when I refused
to pray for myself.

The man asked, then who?
The Prophet said,
Your mother.

Her life flickered
out
before I
was able to
appreciate her.

Mama.

My heart
breaks three
hundred times
over,
because
I didn't listen.

Baby Ghada

I'm going
to name my
Baby girl
Ghada.

And tell her
that it means
Concrete
and steel.

And I'll tell
her it means
Oceans crashing
against rocks.

And I'll tell
Her it means
Hammers

Striking
at anvils.

I'm going to
Name my
Baby girl
Ghada.

And tell her
to wear her name
like a warrior
wears armor.

I'll tell her
to wear her name
like it's an
Undying rose.

Because she
Will be my
Undying rose.

And I'll be the
rocks she crashes
into.

Mama

You, Mama.
Sat with your legs crossed,
and a cup of tea in your hand.
You sipped it through your
crooked teeth.
Laughing at the sound of
Your own jokes that floated
out of your mouth.

You, Mama.
Smoked cigarettes on
California beaches
in the early 1990s.
You leaned your back
against worn out trees
letting the smoke dance around
you.

You, Mama.
Sang songs and screams
with passion.
Your words sprang from your
lips as if they were committing
suicide for leaving you.

You, Mama.
Are me, mama.

I died when you died, mama.
But I'm trying to live, mama.

I promise, mama.
For you, mama.

Spirit

You're sitting beside
yourself.
A body. A Spirit.

I sit next to the
body, under
earth.
under tears.

You place a
hand on my
shoulder.

I only feel
the wind.
And the dirt
grabbing my
fingers.

You're a body
and a Spirit.

I wait.
To join you.

Buried

Sometimes,
I wonder if my
mother
is comfortable
buried in a casket
in New Jersey.

> But it's me
> projecting
> my own
> anxiety because I
> am buried in a
> casket in
> New York.

Roses for Mother's Day

She loved roses.
she had pink and white ones in
our backyard
       she'd stand near the bushes
       and admire them for hours.
       The wind playing with her
hair.

I was never a fan of flowers
Never understood why
people kept them, only to watch
them die.

       My mother always smiled,
       that big smile of hers
whenever
       we brought her roses.

She loved roses
She had pink and white ones
in
our backyard.

Now, I place roses
on her headstone.
Pink and White ones.

Years of Hair and Sorrow

In 1970, she wore her
hair in a bob; the
edges tickled
her jawline, as she
played, barefoot, in her
mother's garden in *Palestine*.

In 1978, she walked
on American soil for the first
time, her hair longer,
catching the tears
as they fell from her face.
She didn't want to be here.

> In 1981, she cut her
> hair short.
> Her smile stretched

from ear to ear
as her fiancé
placed coins of gold
around her neck

In 1988, her hair
grew and flared out
she thought she
was Nouhad Haddad
as she boarded a plane
headed to California.

In 1994, she started
highlighting her black
hair with a hint
of chestnut brown.
The strands slid
down her neck like
a violent rockslide.

In 2007, Her hair began to
fall out.
Pieces falling to the sink
like dying leaves
during New York autumns.

In 2009, her hair
was gray;
it was too short to
catch the tears
that fell from her hollowed eyes.

In 2010, my hair
was too short and the
only thing
catching my tears was
the dirt in a
New Jersey Cemetery.

White Kitten

I saw her.
She was sitting on a chair, alone,
sipping from a cup of tea. A white
kitten danced at her feet.
She was wearing an all white *Thobe*
that was unnaturally clean and her
hair fell to her shoulders. It was jet
black like a starless night and the
wind played with it, tossing it from
side to side, gently.

The sun remained motionless on
the horizon. I couldn't tell if it was
sunrise or sunset. The beams of
light painted the sky purple and
orange. I stood back for a moment
wondering if this whole thing was
a dream or if in fact I had died in

my sleep.
She turned her head to me and smiled. The smile I remembered from my youth. The one that danced on her lips like it didn't have a care in the world. The smile she wore before she was sick. Before we had financial problems. Before I was a college drop out with no real future. It was her one true smile.

I missed that smile. The same smile that said, "you're home, *habibi*."
I walked over to her and sat down on the floor. The white kitten with sky blue eyes came and sat in my lap. It purred.
"He likes you," she said, as she brought the white tea cup to her

lips.

"Hi mama," I said, ignoring the now fast asleep kitten.

"Hi *habibi*," she sang. "I've missed you."

My eyes welled up with tears and I choked on my words, like they were pieces of sweet fruit I swallowed too quickly.

"You don't have to cry here, *omri*," she said, and brushed back my hair with her soft hands. The hands that cradled me when I was a baby.

"Is this a dream," I said, wiping my tears away.

"I don't know." She looked at the sun, which was in the same position as it was earlier.

The sky was still purple and orange. "I miss the sun and its warmth"

"Are you not warm where you are?" I asked, scared for the answer.

"Oh, it is bliss. But there is something about the sun and the way it colors the sky. The way it kisses your skin in the summer." We sat there for a moment, watching the sun's rays bounce and hop on the sky's cloudless dance floor. The kitten was still asleep.

"I don't know what this is, but I hope it never ends," I said. It was a childish thing to say. But my naivety sprang out without my knowing.

"Everything ends, *habibi*," she said.

I waited, thinking she was
going to say something.
Hoping for her to continue.
Waiting for the beautiful
words to leave her lips
giving me warmth, like the
sun.
But I woke up to the sound
of the alarm. I was in my
room again.

She was gone. But there was a
white kitten, sleeping soundly in
my lap.

Boys Don't Cry

Baba came home, his eyes
bloodshot and filled with tears.
He hugged me and I knew.
My legs buckled. He carried my
weight in his arms.

But I couldn't cry.

Baba and I sat alone in the living
room at my aunt's house.
He began sobbing uncontrollably,
Screaming into a pillow,
that matched the tacky sofa.
I held him in my arms as he shook.

But I couldn't cry.

I stood in front of the funeral home,
greeting friends and family.

Men shaking my hands.
Women silently sobbing,
when they saw my face.

But I couldn't cry.

I walked into the room. My
mother's body lying on a steel
table.
I kissed her face.
Said my good byes.
My brother began to cry and I
held him.

But I couldn't cry.

We prayed over her body with a
hundred other men.
The box she was inside was in
front of me.
My brother's body shook.

But I couldn't cry.

We lowered her casket into the
ground. Relatives all around me
tossing handfuls of dirt into my
mother's final resting place.
Muttered prayers in a tongue I
hardly understood.

But I couldn't cry.

I sat alone.
Everyone was gone.
It was just me and
whatever was left
of my mother's spirit.

Finally, I could cry.

I cried for my mama.
I cried for the time spent.
I cried for the time lost.

Home

a.) A dwelling where one
    rests ones head.
b.) A domicile
c.) Abode
d.) Bayt
e.) Mama

She built a house with
her bare hands.
Four walls leaned against
her back.
Her feet were the foundation.
Her legs kept the house from
toppling over.
Her arms kept the roof
over our little hands.

Home is not:

i.)   Building
ii.)   A dwelling
iii.)   Bayt

Home is my mother.
And I am now Homeless.

Blanket

Her hands were
were like the
Blanket that
Khadija wrapped
around the Prophet
when he came back —
from the top of the
Mountain.

*"Allah would
surely protect
him from
any
danger."*

Be

And the Lord said,
"Be and it is."
and my mother
took her
final breath.

Be, and I did.
Be, and she left.

The Lord said,
"Be and it is,"
and I'm trying.

Things I Should Have Said

i. I'm sorry.
> For those moments where
> I was a stupid child.
> When I was wrong but
> I wouldn't admit it.
> For not being there
> when you needed me.
> For not being a better son.
> For not making you proud
> Even though you always
> said you were.

ii. Thank you.
> For all those times you
> helped me, even if you
> had to sacrifice little
> pieces of yourself.

For being you.
For those days you made
me smile when all I
wanted to do was
cry.
For making me
sandwiches with layers
of *labna* and *zaytoon*.
For the times I was sick.
For the times I was healthy

iii. I love you.
When you said it in front
of my friends and I was
too stupid to say it back.
I should have said it more
often than I did.
We had an unspoken
understanding but
I know now that you

would have loved to
hear me say it.

There were a million-
and-one things
I should have said to you,
but I thought you'd live longer.
I thought I had more
time to
tell you all
The Things I should have said.

I'm sorry, mama.
Thank you, mama.
I love you, mama.

Acknowledgements

First and foremost, I would like to thank my mother, without whom I would never have discovered my passion and love for writing. I would also like to thank my friends and family. Your constant support and motivation was the key to this project and I could not have done it without you all.

Thank you.

Lightning Source UK Ltd.
Milton Keynes UK
UKHW03f2213300318
320303UK00001B/140/P